Advance Praise

"As with abstract impressionist painting, the apparent simplicity of the poems in *Hush, Don't Tell Nobody* belie a profound complexity and deep and satisfying richness. This is a major debut, and Kyle Doty is a poet to watch."
> – Charles Blackstone, managing editor of *Bookslut* and author of *Vintage Attraction* and *The Week You Weren't Here*

"Doty's *Hush, Don't Tell Nobody* is a stirring portrait in verse that intimately, with candor and restraint, traces adolescent coming of age within the shadows of abuse. The collection's title appears in four shorter verses as a thread that traces the experience of adolescent physical and emotional violation, confession and absolution, and the eventual forgiveness and redemption of a predator.

The collection is sustained by the poet's observations within the natural world, which serves as a backdrop for adolescent angst and longing in "A Summer Evening in Indiana," where "There's the occasional car that/speeds down the lone country road going/somewhere I'd like to go, because anywhere/would be better than here: eleven and restless/for wild adventure"; other poems explore the fragility of life ("Song for a Bluebird") and majestic power of the natural world to inspire ("A Meal for a Blackbird") and to cleanse ("Tropicalia in Late August"; "Afternoon Storm"). Some verses suggest a marriage of the mundane and the sacred, where conversations with Jesus ("An Average Thursday in Florida") and God ("Voice of God") occur within experiences of daily living. Doty's life as a teacher serves as a window into his awareness of the seemingly unbearable encroaching on childhood ("Elementary K-5") and adolescence ("February 23, Florida"). Ultimately, this collection is a testament to love, redemption, and hope; Doty asks us to connect with our darkest secrets and offer forgiveness to our perpetrators, which, in turn, absolves us. In the concluding poem, "April 26, Edison State College, Rush Library," the speaker addresses his perpetrator: "Do you feel alone?/I hope you don't; I hope you're not./ . . .You're/not alone, not eating TV dinners and watching old episodes of Law and Order SVU,/not torturing yourself for being a monster. You are living; your soul is replenished/because I absolved you from your transgressions."

   – Anne Angstrom, Ph.D., Florida SouthWestern State College

"The greatest artists leave their audience wondering, questioning, feeling. *In Hush Don't Tell Nobody*, Kyle Doty creates this with each poem. I find myself sitting up and noticing a word and wondering, 'Why that word?' At the end of each poem, I find myself wondering, 'Am I right, does it mean this?,' and then reading it again, experiencing each anew each time I read them."

   – Dr. Kim Worth

Hush, Don't Tell Nobody

Hush, Don't Tell Nobody

Kyle Doty

Apprentice House
Loyola University Maryland
Baltimore, Maryland

First Edition

Printed in the United States of America

Paperback ISBN: 978-1-62720-037-0
E-book ISBN: 978-1-62720-038-7

Design by Candis J. Miller
Section icons by creative commons - attribution (CC BY 3.0) the noun project

Published by Apprentice House

Apprentice House
Loyola University Maryland
4501 N. Charles Street
Baltimore, MD 21210
410.617.5265 • 410.617.2198 (fax)
www.apprenticehouse.com
info@apprenticehouse.com

Contents

For Sharayah, always

For Jada, Sariye, and Liam, I love you

Acknowledgements

Continuing gratitude to my parents, John and Phyllis Doty, who always told me to go and do what I love and never settle for less. Thanks also for letting me figure so much out on my own and in my own time.

Thank you to Jacki Lewis, Amanda Bodiot, Ashliegh Kamp, Sarah Robinson, and James Buonocore for reading whenever I asked you to.

Thank you to Nathan and Katie Horst for opening your home and being an unvarying stream of motivation and encouragement to me. Several of these poems were written on your mud porch – for me, a place never void of inspiration.

Thanks to Dr. Anne Angstrom for consistently being a source of encouragement and for making it all look so simple.

Without the initial shock of confidence from Dr. Maria Cahill and Dr. Kim Worth, I would have never begun writing poetry.

Each friend (you know who you are), uniquely special, thank you for the constant stream of love and laughter.

A few of the poems in this book first appeared in the following publications:

- *Illuminatins Literary Review:* "Tropicalia in late August," "A Meal for a Blackbird" both of which also won Edison State College's Rose Koches Poetry Prize.

A Meal for a Blackbird

I envy your aptitude for flight –
your graceful wings, soft feathers
glistening in rain – blue, green,
immaculate gold. The way

you swoop to supple earth
from depressed summer sky –
icy raindrops a reminder of the
languid winter.

You power a worm from his
murky domicile with your sharp
beak – the color of desert
stone.

You take flight lifting
from earth with grace like
a noble deer. I linger, waiting
to hear your wild cry.

An Average Thursday in Florida

Today I woke up before sunrise and made coffee,
ate two pieces of toast and some watermelon, and
then put on a pair of slack pants – too baggy in the
legs, too short.

At work I sat around and talked to books, listened to
author's whispers from behind the hard covers.

When I came home, I sat down on the tattered sofa where
I sometimes sleep and had a conversation with Jesus.
After a while, after the sun had gone down
and the day was reduced to a faint glow, I asked the Lord if
he'd multiply the fish in the freezer; he shrugged his
narrow shoulders and turned his ruined palms skyward
and said, "why not?"

I'm declaring a war on apathy!

– Dr. Kim Worth, year 1999/2000, 9th grade Drama teacher.

I hope for rain in the evening,

for clear sky to give way
to low-hanging clouds, black

like rotten fruit swaying from
summer Maples. I ask for wind –

tempest strength – and the crooked
rod of electricity that cuts through

twilight. For the sound of thunder
like a herd of elephants trampling

from the distance.

I pray for a storm that cleanses,
like wire brush on metal,

the ebony mood of indifference.

Song for a Bluebird

How is she? he asks.
His skin hangs from bulldog
jowls and jiggles like
pale Jell-O.
I know the *She* of whom he
cautiously inquires –
a daughter.
A father's anxiety
encrypted in his eyes:
watery dull blue that hardly
hints at a life lived.
I don't say, *you must feel helpless.*
I say, *she's good, and*
    I'm proud of her.
He's proud too, but troubled.
She's been dumped and
cataloged too many bruises for
him to relax.
Her own daughter took pictures
of bruises in the bathroom here. He
points behind him with his thumb
and sighs.
What it must be like to be father
of a woman interrupted. *She's a*
fighting soul, he tells me. *She'll*
make it. A father's hope.
She will, I say, being
the voice of his optimism.
He settles back into his chair
and whistles a tune for the

bluebird that sits on the roof
of the newly painted but
crumbling shed.
The fragile bird sings back
a song of redemption,
and I wonder if the old man
hasn't just tried to call
his little girl home.

for Renee

Summer Evening in Indiana

The sun as a fireball descends just past
the other side of the dried up field giving
 the air around eleven-year-old me a gauzy
quality – hot haze streams up from summer
scorched earth,

and I sit on the deck in front of our country
home and listen to the
cicadas' chorus begin their warm up
for their nightly orchestra performance.
There's the occasional car that
speeds down the lone country road going

somewhere I'd like to go, because anywhere
would be better than here: eleven and restless
for wild adventure. Frogs from the dry creek bed
start up next, and a bird's wings thrash overhead
while I listen to the groan the moon makes as

it pulls itself up from somewhere across
an ocean I've never seen and won't see
for several years. The neighbor steps
out of her ancient farm house and crosses
the sparse yard to the barn to haul sacks
of chicken feed and bales of hay to feed

the enormous brown horses. Not even with the sun
disappearing does it get even a little cooler.
I stay in my spot and focus on the darkening

sky, try to remember where grandma taught
me the Big Dipper would turn up. All I want
is to be in the airplane that's crossing the

sky, heading east, going somewhere big
where there are no farms, or livestock, or
cicadas. You told me the other night
that our secret made us strange, that what I
let you do made us queer. I close my eyes
to still the terror. Deep breaths. Deep breaths.
The chickens across the yard bubble and cluck

while they scratch the dusty earth looking for feed
and insects, the only aspiration of their short
lives. The veiled moon is full in the sky
breathing in the last of the sun's light.
As the cicadas begin
their first aria, mom switches on the living
room lamp spilling yellow light through
the window, washing my body along with the
weathered planks of the deck.

Tropicalia in Late August

This morning I stepped out
expecting a wave of humid air
and large, buzzing bugs. I was surprised
when a breeze tagged my bare skin;
it felt like fall foreshadowing winter.

I nodded to the breeze which was still
waking up and whispered my thanks.
It replied by interrupting the branches
on the tree out front, startling some
young birds.

You're welcome, the bluebirds sang,
as though they could interpret the
tongue of the wind.

Adolescent in Suburbia

A barefoot boy walks down a typical suburban street
at twilight.
Summertime has only just begun, the air turned warm
not a week ago.

A woman stands naked in her window.

The boy sees, shifts his eyes quickly.
The image frightens him; he's never encountered
such beauty.

Something about the picture that's been burned
into his cerebral cortex makes an odd sort of sense.

Street lamps switch on as the sun blazes the sky pink
and orange and violet, and the boy goes home to dinner,
where after, he asks questions about
women and anatomy
that makes his mother blush,

      his father swell with pride.

Afternoon Storm

Pregnant clouds come in from the gulf announcing their
labor much the way women do when they're ready:
A low grumble, an ominous face. The flies swarm ahead of
the rain, hundreds of them. We can't open the door without
them getting inside and defiling our food, leaving their pinprick
marks on the walls, the lampshades.

This is my favorite time of day. The rain washes away the heat,
chases away the humidity. I always hope for hail and lightning –
A tornado to slither like an evil snake across the sky so I can
witness the power of God and go to bed feeling like I've seen something.

Hush, Don't Tell Nobody

Midnight in the Kitchen of Good and Evil

i. The light from the kitchen
   beats back midnight –
   everyone's asleep, but I'm
   standing bare-foot on the blue linoleum floor.
   The pattern reminds me of stones
   in a river, and I'm talking to a
   whisper of a man. I'm feeling sick, my nine-
   year-old body trembling, my skinny,
   pale legs sticking out of black
   Budweiser shorts like Jell-O.
   You can't tell anyone our secret, he says.

You can't tell a soul.

Dinner

Slowly I pour rice into boiling water. I pour
slowly because when I just dump it in, into the hot,
rolling sea of tap, the rice clumps like a soft bit of clay.

I scoop out giant mounds of white grains into wooden
bowls, the ones my wife got on sale at Goodwill and
add sea salt and hot sauce – the meal of poor people.

From outside, my son sits on the swing hung
from the tree and blows me a kiss. He already ate: Steel
Cut Oats with raisins and brown sugar. He meows at the cat,

sings to himself a little song the way young children do. When
I look out again he's on top of the car, and there's a lightning
storm coming. I walk to the window and motion for him to get

down; he only smiles at me. I have to go outside and tell him,
explain the danger of Florida Lightning.

After the rice, I look for something sweet and find
an orange package of peanut butter cups. By instinct my
hand reaches out to clasp the shiny package between my
fingers, but I stop myself.

I remember my tooth decay and

that the candy is for the kids.

April 12, 2014, Florida

At the onset of summer's fever
I prepare by imagining myself at
the base of a snowy mountain –
large Evergreens with frosty tips towering
over me, and I listen for the susurration
of starry night sky or the song of dying
wildflowers warbling their own version
of the Kaddish.

I stand at the edge of our yard
my arms raised above my head and

howl a war cry: my elegy to winter.

The Day I Realized You're Only Human

I changed into your clothes
at your request. Bright red briefs, two sizes too big...
because you were seventeen and I was only eleven.
They were red and reminded me of superman. I wore your t-shirt,
too. We had just come in from the rain, the two of us
out searching for snakes along the trails near the elementary school,
    searching
for railroad ties along the nearly-forgotten tracks. Some nights the sound
of a ghost train would blow its hollow haunted whistle as I drifted off to
    sleep.
We were wet from head to toe, and that was how I came to wear your
    underwear, your
t-shirt. Your lusty stare cut through my body and burned holes in my
    eyes.

Later, when we were dry and the adults (weren't you one by then?) sat
in the kitchen clutching mugs of steaming instant coffee and eating sweet
bread and cookies, you took back your clothing; and with an anxious grin
asked me if I wanted to "you know..."
I said I didn't, and your face fell.
I felt for the first time what it must be like to be you:
A crushed flower under the heel of an elephant.

Elementary K – 5

I.

Devin. Little boy who asked me to play
basketball. You noticed my tattoos and told
me that your dad is a tattoo artist. When I asked
you where he works you told me *from home. He
charges twenty-five dollars.*

You told me with a smile (dull, crooked teeth)
that your favorite colors are pink and purple.
You like dressing in Camo and going to the ACT Shelter–
Abuse Counseling and Treatment.

II.

Boy under the pavilion,
I wonder what it's like
For you never having
Heard your mother say
I love you.
Never being able to trust
Your big brother or
His friends.
Never hearing your
Father say he's proud,
But only that he's going

To beat your ass.

III.

Little girl with braces on
your legs, your lip ruined,
your mind soft.
Thank you for taking me by
the hand and smiling at me.
Your small, pretty eyes sparkled,
and when you spoke, you said,
daddy.
You melted this heart that had
somehow turned to stone somewhere
along the way.

IV.

Put the books in order, the old
library volunteer told me.
[   ]
*The kids never put the books back
right.*
[   ]
You want to be a teacher?
[   ]

*Kids these days can't learn; no
one can teach kids to learn.*

The library was empty,
Not a student in sight.

V.

There are always teacher assistants:
College students wanting experience,
Older people hoping to make a difference.
This one, she was on her phone a lot,
trying to clear her name from the night
before.
I'm hung over, she said.
And I didn't steal the pot from that house—
I can't smoke right now. I have a good job.

Hush, Don't Tell Nobody

Whispered prayers

ii. Don'tlet-itbe,God.

Dont'LetWhatHeSaysBeTrue.

Hush, Don't Tell Nobody

iii. Hush,

don't tell

nobody,

he said.

.

Four Points by Sheraton, Savannah, GA

There's a flood warning just to the north and east, still within Savannah
city limits, and I keep looking out the window which overlooks E. Bay
    Street
where semi-trucks belch by and car's horns shout their warnings, and I
    check
out the massive bridge that spans the Savannah River. I want to see if
    the
water is where it was last night – tucked safely between its banks.
The weatherman says it's nearly at flood stage, only about a foot
more to rise before some streets are impassable. We're here in our
hotel; Sharayah's checking messages, I'm in a towel fresh from the
shower, watching her. Her hair is like a lion's mane in the morning,
her eyes dark and sexy. Soon we're going to brunch and then down
to that lazy, passive aggressive river to watch the container ships chug by
    and
feed the birds that frequent the Riverwalk.

Indiana

Fields pregnant with corn and soy beans
dancing in warm-going-cool breeze; the
endless stretches of cracked earth gasping for water
demanding the petulant blue sky for just a drop.

This is Indiana.

A lone farmhouse at the end of an august country road,
families' livelihoods on either side of the solitary stretch –
(the same place dad got out and peed next to the idling Ram
and chose another beer from the cooler in the tool box). The sun
reflects off the front window and bathes the bloodshot bricks in
autumn evening.

I knew the boy who lived in the house, the son of a farmer. I
wrote him a love note in sixth grade when I learned how to cut
with words, my pencil a weapon; I persuaded him
to come the next day dressed in a suit and to bring flowers
and candy. He came, and because he was fat and wanted a friend,
he dressed in Sunday Best and brought the recommended treats.

Oh how we laughed.

For years after, whenever I'd see that house, I thought about
the boy and the note, the flowers hanging in his chubby hands,
his plump fingers gripping the bright chocolate box, and I wondered
if he hated me

or if his father had taught him to forgive hate mongers and browbeaters; that those who taunt others are often haunted by someone else.

Painting of a Balloon Man

In my hand – the one I use to write with –
I hold a bouquet of colorful balloons and
walking down the center of the street, into
the sunset, I easily skip and click my heels
together like I've seen old men do in movies.

Why the joy, you ask?

       I don't know.

It's just the picture I've been staring at
the last few days – the picture from the
place in my mind where pictures like this
come from.

I sat down on this rainy afternoon with a
cup of tea to paint the picture using syntax –
my wife would use brush and acrylic.

The reason for the joy is unclear, but
finally I see the whole picture. The balloons
have picked me up and slowly, eternally
slow, I float up and up into the sunset
and float away over the ocean.

The Fire Alarm

shouted its warning at
3 A.M. Five strident screams
cut through the somnolence
raising me from the sofa.

Smell of smoke absent,
I wondered if it hadn't been
a dream –

or perhaps an angel
with an immaculate silver
sword to deliver me
a message from heaven.

Blessed is Bliss

not hearing I love you
        but
I don't love you anymore
        is
the first clue;
        or
is it the absence
        of
a smile when I walk in the room
        or
when I discover the alternate email account
        or
the private, giggly phone calls
        and
the new shampoo, the wardrobe?

I question myself, say, while walking
the dog: Am I being paranoid?

When I'm at lunch with a friend
from college and he offers this
advice: Ignorance is bliss. I believe
him
        because

it is, after all, bliss. I'm alive,
anyway; I'm alive, and that's bliss.

for a coworker

Voice of God

Down the
sidewalk –
the tree lined
one near
the campus
library I like
to wander
down – I heard
a whisper wind
its way through
the trees and
land on my
shoulder.
It was the
voice of the
Almighty
filling the
silence besides
the tip tap
of my vintage
Nikes on the
pavement.
I'm here,
I heard Him
say. I'm here,
and I'm willing
to arm wrestle.

Hush, Don't Tell Nobody

Confessions

iv.

After vacation with family from Miami –
Branson, MO in the middle of October,
a missed day of 5th grade, I whispered strange
secrets into my mother's ear and slept like a baby
after.

      In the still of the night when I was foggy
with sleep she woke me with a message
from Dad: it's not your fault.

I had been dreaming of soldiers. Tall
ones with grey hats and coats with
tails.

Two Mexicans

Bright-eyed, fresh morning,
Sky pure like water.
Sun up, building in intensity–
Higher and hotter, higher and hotter.

The worries on my anxious mind
Swell: our bank is the catacombs,
The car's on fumes, and the opulently decorated
Tree at home is naked under its pre-lit boughs.

I see two Mexican's crossing the road.
A woman and a man, bright-eyed and
Fresh. Their box truck parked on the shoulder
With its flashers anxiously blinking.

They've stopped for coffee, and now they
Are returning. Back to work, back to the
Rush of the morning. I've forged ahead,
Pointing my car towards the endless miles
Of highway before I realize what I saw:

Love.

He bought her coffee at rush hour on a
Cool, bright-eyed morning and parked
The box truck on the shoulder. He led her
Safely across and back again and probably
Fought for a space – a tiny singular unit of
Area – to maneuver his truck towards the
Miles of endless highway ahead.

Stretched out in bed this morning,

warm down cover atop the cool
sheet keeping my long, raw body
concealed from the humid
chill of the first day of spring.

I think about love. What mystery!
I apprize my wife's numinous
Touch.

    Our legs intertwined,
the gentle round of my foot
resting in the yawning arc of hers,

        our cold bodies

            warming one another.

My front to her bottom like
two parenthesis.
Masculine and feminine –
Tristan and Isolde.

Tonight I wrote you a letter

Five pages double-spaced,
ten point font, Times New

Roman. It's hard to believe nineteen
years filled the pages. It would seem

to take more, possibly written on legal
sized, heavy, quality threaded paper,

but five was all it took, written with venom
and love. I forgave you formally tonight;

the letter my speech and my prayer along
with a gift telling you I forgive you. Exonerating

you took time and work and trust that what
I'm letting go will set me free like the reckless

wind of a tempest stampeding onto Florida's shore.

February 23, Florida

It's two days before my day of birth,
and my mother just shared a cute picture
of me at three. I'm wearing a little boy's
business suit that would be popular today. The other picture she chose
was one from
my adolescent era – strange hair, oily skin, and awkward.

The picture reminded me of a student –
A tall lanky boy, fourteen, with the brightest
bluest eyes I've ever seen.

His mother left him on a stranger's doorstep
before Christmas.
Two weeks ago the woman, the stranger, set him
free in the care of a school social worker – "he's too expensive."

How is a boy like that supposed to make it?

I can see him in the back seat of the state-owned sedan,
his azure eyes searching the scorched winter landscape,
and I feel the heaviness in his narrow chest, the petulant anxiety
in his naïve mind. His light eyes close;
    the image behind them a vacant
idea of future.

for a former student

Hush, Don't Tell Nobody

Metal Mouth

v.

Though we weren't
Catholic, my post-confession
remedy similar to Rosary was to stare
into the dark metallic barrel
of a Remington and pray.

Solely cerebral,
my tongue still recoiled from the
strong metallic tang of death.

April 26, Edison State College, Rush Library

Late afternoon, trees just budding, awakening from the harsh winter you
  had this year,
and I'm here in Florida where the trees are starting to turn; we get fall in
  late spring.
The leaves from the tree in my front yard crunch under my bare feet in
  the morning
when I step out with my coffee to sample the day. Like me, you're
  probably at work

doing whatever it is that you do to keep the paychecks coming. I wonder
  if maybe we're
both looking out the window at the same time, appreciating spring,
  somehow
together, as if the earth or fate or God has chanced us to simultaneously
  experience the
intimacy of changing seasons – nothing wholly un-similar to seeing a
  woman change from

bedclothes to fresh skirt – and I can't help but wonder, in this hushed
  moment, if you
think of me from time to time. Do you wonder who I became since you
  last saw me? On
the floor, looking up at you, nearly twelve years old and terrified at what
  you said the
night before in the kitchen – because I let you do that thing to me, you
  said, we were strange.
I wonder if you sit at a desk like I do while you work. A window near you
  where

Kyle Doty 57

perhaps a car drives by or a man walking his dog; I picture a small one, a
      beagle, perhaps,
and if those people know what you've done, as if by some force of ESP or
      of a kind of
animal-sense instinct they can detect a predator. Do you feel alone?

I hope you don't; I hope you're not.

Sometimes I imagine you walking up to your home, a townhouse on the
      rougher
side of town because no one on the better side would accept your
      background
check; and when you turn the frigid bronze door handle – it's always
      winter – there's
a woman who smiles at you, welcomes you home, and a big dog who
      wants his
head patted, for you to scratch in that perfect place behind his ears. You're
not alone, not eating TV dinners and watching old episodes of Law and
      Order SVU,
not torturing yourself for being a monster. You are living; your soul is
      replenished

because I absolved you from your transgressions.

Apprentice House is the country's only campus-based, student-staffed book publishing company. Directed by professors and industry professionals, it is a nonprofit activity of the Communication Department at Loyola University Maryland.

Using state-of-the-art technology and an experiential learning model of education, Apprentice House publishes books in untraditional ways. This dual responsibility as publishers and educators creates an unprecedented collaborative environment among faculty and students, while teaching tomorrow's editors, designers, and marketers.

Outside of class, progress on book projects is carried forth by the AH Book Publishing Club, a co-curricular campus organization supported by Loyola University Maryland's Office of Student Activities.

Eclectic and provocative, Apprentice House titles intend to entertain as well as spark dialogue on a variety of topics. Financial contributions to sustain the press's work are welcomed. Contributions are tax deductible to the fullest extent allowed by the IRS.

To learn more about Apprentice House books or to obtain submission guidelines, please visit www.apprenticehouse.com.

Apprentice House
Communication Department
Loyola University Maryland
4501 N. Charles Street
Baltimore, MD 21210
Ph: 410-617-5265 • Fax: 410-617-2198
info@apprenticehouse.com • www.apprenticehouse.com

www.ingramcontent.com/pod-product-compliance
Lightning Source LLC
LaVergne TN
LVHW051429080426
835508LV00022B/3310